ANDROID TESTING MADE EASY

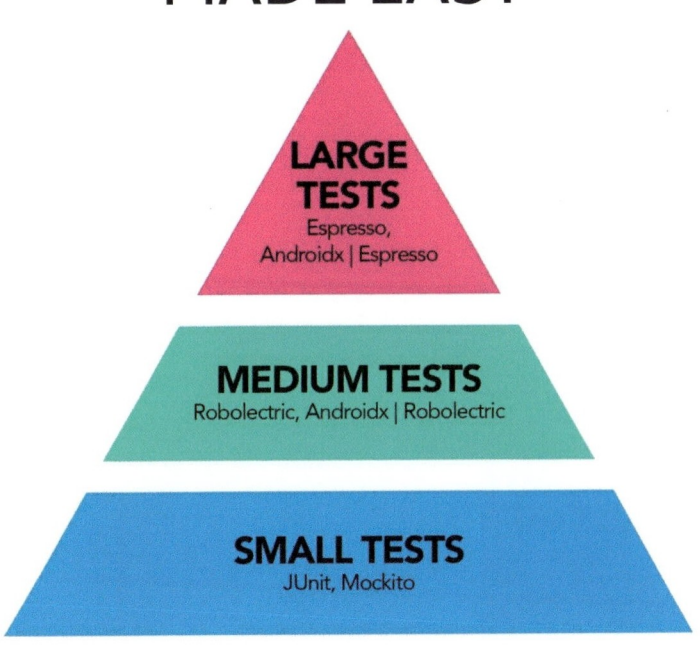

LARGE TESTS
Espresso, Androidx | Espresso

MEDIUM TESTS
Robolectric, Androidx | Robolectric

SMALL TESTS
JUnit, Mockito

By
Marc Daniel Registre

© Copyright 2021 by Marc Daniel Registre - All rights reserved.

It is not legal to reproduce, duplicate, or transmit any part of this document in electronic means or printed format. Recording of

MARC DANIEL REGISTRE

this publication is strictly prohibited.

I dedicate this book to:

My lovely wife, Christina Phara Registre, who has been by my side for quite some time and has provided a lot of support. And my parents, Joseph and Florence Registre, for all their help.

TABLE OF CONTENTS

Introduction

Part I: Test Environment

Chapter One: Android Test Directories

PART II: Small Test
    Android Test Tools

Chapter Two: Unit Tests (JUnit)
    What is Unit Testing?

    Setting Up Unit Tests

    Unit Under Test

    Testing Unit Under Test

    Understanding Unit Under Test

    Table 1. JUnit Assert Table

    Table 2: JUnit Annotations Table

    Chapter Summary

Chapter Three: Unit Test (Mockito Library)
    What is Mockito

    Setting up Mockito

    Unit Under Test

    Testing Unit Under Test - Mockito

    Understanding Unit Under Test-Mockito

    Table 3: Mockito Annotations

    Chapter Summary

PART III: Medium Test
    Android Test Tools

Chapter Four: Integration Tests (Robolectric)

What are Integration Tests?

Using Robolectric

Setup Integration Test

Unit Under Test

Testing Integration Test - Robolectric

Understanding Integration Test - Robolectric

Table 4: Robolectric Annotations Table

Chapter Summary

Chapter Five: Integration Tests (Androidx | Robolectric)
Androidx

Androidx | Robolectric

Section 1: Testing Activity with ActivityScenario

Testing Integration Test - Androidx | Robolectric

Understanding Integration Test - Androidx | Robolectric

Section 2: Testing Activity with *ActivityScenarioRule*

Understanding ActivityScenarioRule Test

Section 3: Testing Fragments (FragmentScenario)

FragmentScenarios Testing

Understanding FragmentScenarios

Chapter Summary

Part IV: Large Tests
User Interface Testing

Android Test Tools

Chapter Six: User Interface Tests (Espresso)
Espresso

The basics of an espresso test are as follows:

Chapter Summary

Chapter Seven: User Interface Tests (Androidx | Espresso)
The basics of an espresso test are as follows:

Espresso Setup

- ViewMatchers
- ViewActions
- Table 6: ViewActions commonly used:
- ViewAssertions
- Table 7: *ViewAssertion* table
- Chapter Summary

Conclusion
Acknowledgments
Editors
About the Author

INTRODUCTION

Congratulations on buying the book that will make you a better-skilled software engineer. A software engineer must understand how software systems work together, optimize them, and design systems to avoid potential issues. Users interact with an app on various levels; thus, a developer should test multiple use cases and interactions.

What is a Test
A test is a procedure used to evaluate if the system works as expected. Manual/Automated Testing ensures the implementation of requirements and the assurance that the tests will work as per the users' expectations.

Why is Testing necessary
Defects or failures can occur at any stage during the software development cycle. Software engineers test to identify various kinds of faults, reduce flaws, and increase the system's overall quality before using the product. Every code that a software engineer creates needs Testing. A thoroughly tested software ensures reliability, quality, and high performance of the software operation.

What should you test
Tests should focus on behaviors, and behaviors are to be tested independently from one another.

This book is for the Java/Kotlin developer who has experience in coding and design and would like to learn the science behind Testing and strengthen their testing skills.

Please don't wait to read this book; designed to be an essential how-to, compact, and straight-to-point point.

Android Test Tools

SMALL TESTS
JUnit, Mockito

JUnit
JUnit is a unit-testing framework that is simple and convenient. The APIs allow one to write tests and perform common testing operations such as setup, teardown, and assertions. Chapter 2 focuses on Unit Tests.

Mockito
The purpose of unit tests is to test a code in isolation from any of its dependencies. Mockito helps mock these dependencies. Chapter 3 focuses on Mockito Testing.

Chapter Two: Unit Tests (Junit)

SMALL TESTS
JUnit

What is Unit Testing?

Unit Testing is the first level of Testing done in software testing, and they are the minor kind of Test to write. The purpose of unit testing is to validate that each unit or method (the smallest unit of code) performs as expected.

All code is unsafe until it is unit tested. Every new piece of code or logic added should be unit tested. The unit test should be done independently or isolated from the environment and other parts.

Unit tests are to be done by the developer who created the code. This type of Testing is known as white box testing. In White-Box Testing, the tester understands the code implementation's ins and outs writes the code for each unit or method created. The developer also provides the inputs and verifies if the expected output is correct.

As stated above, a developer has done unit tests to prove that a piece of code does what the developer intends it to do. Unit tests focus only on a particular piece of code while ignoring the plethora of methods around it. Unit tests allow one to test beyond normal operation limits so that the method is robust and does not break under different inputs.

Good unit test coverage increases confidence in changing and maintaining the code. As you make code changes, you will be able to catch defects introduced into the codebase.

Setting Up Unit Tests

Open *app/build.gradle* file and add the following dependency:

```
dependencies {
    ...
    testImplementation("junit:junit:
                                    <version>")
    ...
}
```

Where should the Test be located

Typically, unit tests are created in a separate project or source folder to keep the test code apart from the real code. The standard convention from the Gradle build tools is to use the following folder structure:

- *src/test/kotlin* - test classes
- *src/main/kotlin* - production code

Unit Under Test

For example, you have a class called *MyAccount.kt*, which contains a method:

fun createNewAccount(val name: String): Boolean

```kotlin
class MyAccount() {

    fun createNewAccount(
        val name: String
    ) : Boolean {

        return true
    }
}
```

Testing Unit Under Test

src/test/MyAccountTest.kt

```kotlin
class MyAccountTest {

    lateinit var myAccount : MyAccount

    @Before
    fun setUp() {

        myAccount= MyAccount()

    }

    @Test
    fun shouldReturnTrue
        WhenNewAccountCreatedTest() {

        val isAccountCreated = myAccount
            .createNewAccount("mdr123")

        Assert
        .assertTrue(isAccountCreated)
    }

    @After
    fun teardown() {
        myAccount = null
```

Understanding Unit Under Test

1. When naming the test class, a widely used convention is to have the "Test" sufix at the end of the test class names.

```
Class MyAccountTest {..
```

The test suffix emphasizes the object's responsibilities, making it easier for future engineers who want to know what it does without delving into the code.

2. A test's name should convey the meaning of the code that it's testing.

```
fun shouldReturnTrue
WhenNewAccountCreatedTest() {...
```

3. The Test should contain the following structure

Given[the input]
   The condition
When[method called]
   Action taken
Then[the expected result]
   Asserted to be true

4. Every Test should have the following format:

Setup -> Assertion -> Teardown

Setup

Inside setup is where the common object between test cases goes. Usually, you would find the instantiation of the class that is under Test inside the setup method. Once the class instantiates, its methods are exposed.

In this step, you instantiate the class that is under Test to expose the methods.

```
...
@Before
fun setUp() {
    myAccount= MyAccount(user)
}
...
```

JUnit 4 Annotation : **@Before**

@Before
It is executed before each Test. Prepare the test environment (e.g., initialize the class)

*See Annotation Table at the end of chapter

Assertion

Execute the method and verify that the method is doing what you are expecting it to do.

```kotlin
@Test
fun shouldReturnTrue
    WhenNewAccountCreatedTest() {

    val isAccountCreated = myAccount
        .createNewAccount("mdr123")

    Assert
    .assertTrue(isAccountCreated)
}
```

Assert Statements
assertTrue(boolean condition)

Assert.assertTrue
Checks that the Boolean condition is true.

*See Assert Statements Table at the end of the chapter.

Tear-Down

Clean up the code, breaking down any common objects that need to be released.

```kotlin
@Test
fun teardown() {
    myAccount = null
```

JUnit 4 Annotation : **@After**

@After
Executed after each Test. It can be used to delete temporary data, restore defaults, and cleans up the environment.

*See Annotation Table at the end of chapter

JUnit Asserts

All of the assert methods listed below will report a pass if the assertion is true or fail if the assertion is false. Once one Test encounters a failure (failed assert), it will continue to run if there are other tests inside the test class.

Table 1. Junit Assert Table

assertEquals(expected: Object, actual: Object) **assertEquals(expected: long, actual: long)** **assertEquals(expected: float, actual: float)** **assertEquals(expected: double, actual: double)**	
Asserts that the expected and the actual objects are equal. *Expected*: the expected value that you would have to write. *Actual*: the value to check against the expected, which is the code's value under Test.	
assertFalse(value: Boolean)	
Assert that the value is false.	
assertTrue(value: Boolean)	
Assert that the value is true.	
assertNotEquals(expected: Object, actual: Object)	
Assert that the expected value is not equal to the actual value.	
assertNotNull(value: Object)	
Assert that the value is not null.	
assertSame(expected: Object, actual: Object)	
Asserts that the expected and actual value are the same object.	
assertThrows(expected : Class<T>, runnable:ThrowingRunnable)	
Assert that the runnable throws an exception.	
Fail(message: String)	

Table 2: Junit Annotations Table

@Test
This annotation indicates that the methods that follow, in the following line, should be executed as a test case.
@Before
This annotation is where instantiation of the class happens. Its runs before every Test.
@After
@After annotation runs after each Test; to reset memory, variables, etc.
@BeforeClass
If several tests share expensive data computations, such instantiation is done here.
@AfterClass
If *BeforeClass* has extensive computations or allocates external resources, those resources are released here.
@Ignore
Ignore the Test that this is attached to.

Chapter Summary

Unit test is the first level of Testing done in software testing.

- Unit Test is the first level of Testing done in software testing. Its purpose is to test application logic.
- Unit tests should be done independently or isolated from the environment and other parts.
- When naming the test class, a widely used convention is to have the "Test" suffix at the end of the test class names.

```
class MyAccountTest { ...
```

- Every Test Should have the following format
  Setup:

  Instantiation/Initialize the common objects needed during Testing.

  Assert:

  Verification of the state

  Teardown:

  Clean up any allocated resources or memory

In the next chapter, you will learn about Mockito Library used in Unit testing. Use Mockito when you are dealing with external dependencies to your unit testing. The next chapter will help you understand how to tackle external dependencies in your Testing.

Chapter Three: Unit Test (Mockito Library)

SMALL TESTS
Mockito

What is Mockito

The previous chapter stated that unit testing needs to be isolated. We should only be testing one unit at a time. In this case, one method at a time, as a method is the smallest unit possible. Once your Test starts relying on another class or method (external dependencies), it is no longer a unit test.

Mockito comes into play when you have a method that has a dependency on another. Mocking is creating an object that implements the behavior of a dependent subunit.

Setting up Mockito

Open app/build.gradle file and add the following dependency:

```
dependencies {
    testImplementation `junit:junit:
                                    <version>'

    testImplementation
            'org.mockito:Mockito-core:
                                    <version>'

    testImplementation
            'org.mockito:mockito-inline:
                                    <version>'
}
```

Note: Since Mockito version 1 cannot mock/spy the following: Final classes, anonymous classes, primitive types, use mockito version 2 or higher.

createNewAccount() method depends on *isUserVerify()*, in order to test the creation of a new account. As a result, you would have to mock the *isUserVerify()*; so it returns a specific value to focus Testing on createNewAccount().

Unit Under Test

```kotlin
class User {
    fun isUserVerified(): Boolean {
        return true
    }
}
```

```kotlin
class MyAccount(val user: User) {
    /*
     * Takes in an account and returns true if the
     * account was created successfully, and
     * false otherwise.
     */
    fun createNewAccount(
        val name: String
    ): Boolean {

        if (user.isUserVerified()) {
            return true
        }

        return false
    }
}
```

MyAccount Class has a method that uses another method in the *User* class; this is called a **Dependency**.

As stated above, a Unit Test tests specific methods' behavior without relying on their dependencies' behavior. We mock the dependency to define its behavior.

Testing Unit Under Test - Mockito

src/test/MyAccountTest.kt

```kotlin
class MyAccountTest {

    val user: User = mock(User::class.java)

    lateinit var myAcc : MyAccount

    @Before
    fun setUp() {
        myAcc = MyAccount(user)
    }

    @Test
    fun should_return_true_
            when_new_account_created()
     {
      `when`(user.isUserVerified())
       .thenReturn(true)

       val isCreateAccGood =
         myAcc.createNewAccount("mdr123")

       Assert
        .assertTrue(isCreateAccountGood)
    }
```

```kotlin
@Test
fun should_return_false_
     when_new_account_created() {

   `when`(user.isUserVerified())
   .thenReturn(true)

   val isCreateAccGood =
    myAcc.createNewAccount("mdr123")

   Assert
   .assertFalse(isCreateAccountGood)
 }
}
```

Understanding Unit Under Test-Mockito

1. A Mock object User created.

```kotlin
val user: User = mock(User::class.java)
```

2. Inside the setup function, we instantiate MAcount(User),passing the constructor's mocked User.

```kotlin
@Before
fun setUp() {
    myAcc = MyAccount(user)
}
```

Once we pass the User's mock instance, we can now have any method inside the User class return fake/dummy objects.

2. A mocked object User allows us to return dummy data. That dummy data returns Boolean true

```kotlin
`when`(user.isUserVerified())
                        .thenReturn(true)
```

Since User is being mocked, using `when`(<method>).thenReturn(<value>). We are making the <method> to always return the <value> we specified.
The purpose of mocking is to eliminate testing all the dependencies of a class or function, so your tests are more focused and more straightforward in what they are trying to prove.

Table 3: Mockito Annotations

@Mock	
	The *@Mock* annotations create a mocked instance. Mock objects created with the *@Mock* do not maintain the state changes to the object.
@Spy	
	The @Spy annotation creates an actual instance of the class and maintains the state changes. The difference between Mock vs. Spy is that Spy maintains states while Mock does not.
@Captor	
	Captures an argument passed to a method to inspect it.
@InjectMocks	
	Inject mock field into the object under Test.

Chapter Summary

Mocks allow for isolating a method and testing it without interacting with external dependencies.

Spy and Mocks are similar, and the difference is that Spy maintains the state changes, while Mock does not.

Example mocking *User::class.java*

```kotlin
val user: User = mock(User::class.java)
```

Unit tests only test pieces of the code individually. While unit tests increase the code's quality and safeguard when refactoring code, they only isolate components in isolation. The next chapter focuses on testing how different parts of your code interact with one another.

PART III: MEDIUM TEST

Although small tests are fast and focused, allowing you to address failures quickly, they are also low-fidelity and self-contained, making it challenging to have confidence that a passing test allows your app to work. A medium test typically covers a larger volume of your system than a single-class test, so it is more efficient.

In Android, medium testing is integration testing. Integration testing usually involves two or more components/modules/features interacting with one another. As you create new features or modules into the code base, they will be medium tested to ensure they work with other modules in the system as expected.

Integration or medium Testing tests the behavior of the modules as a unit.

Writing integration tests increases the coverage and improves the reliability of the tests.

Android Test Tools

MEDIUM TESTS
Robolectric, Androidx | Robolectric

Robolectric

Robolectric test is run Android tests on your local machine, allowing the Android API to configure to the desired conditions. Chapter 6 focuses on Robolectric.

Robolectric | Androidx

Robolectric is compatible with Android official testing libraries. Chapter 5 focuses on Robolectric when it comes to androidx, as AndroidX Test is the new way of testing code that interacts with the Android framework.

Chapter Four: Integration Tests (Robolectric)

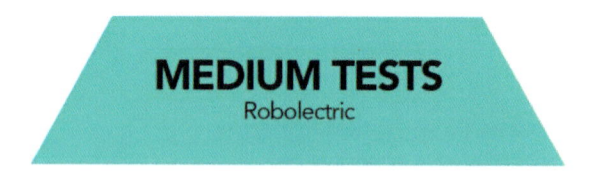

What are Integration Tests?

Integration testing is a type of Testing where software modules are integrated logically and tested as a group. Software projects almost always consist of different modules, and more than one engineer or programmer can write these modules. These modules should be tested and confirmed that they operate in unity. The best way to do integration testing is to test modules that are logically related to each other.
Using Robolectric

Robolectric has evolved to be more of an integration testing tool best suited to test how our module interacts with one another and the Android Framework. Robolectric is a framework that allows the developer to focus on the behavior of the application. Robolectric mocks the view interactions of the Android SDK framework APIs.

With Robolectric:
- We can test Android components in isolation, such as Views, Fragments, Bundle, Intent, and much more.
- We can perform actions on *view* objects.
- Android Resources can load for Testing.

Robolectric mocks the Android framework, allowing it to test on the JVM without an emulator or device.

Setup Integration Test

JUnit dependency allows for the annotations and assertions during the Test. Robolectric enables the Test to run on the Java Virtual Machine, allowing one to test how it interacts with the Android API.

```
android {
    testOptions {
        unitTests {
            includeAndroidResources = true
        }
    }
}

dependencies {

testImplementation 'junit:junit:<version>'

testImplementation 'org.robolectric:robolectric:<version>'

}
```

Unit Under Test

Let's say we have *AccountActivity*, which interacts with an SQLite database called *AccountDatabase* and navigates to an *AcctDetailsActivity*.

Since integration testing is necessary to verify that the software modules work in unity, we will test:
- How does AccountActivity work with AcccountDetailsActivity in unity?
  module #1 -> module #2

- AccountActivity interaction with AccountDatabase.

module #1 -> module #3

Module#1 - Account class

AccountActivity has two buttons. When clicked, it navigates to another Activity. The second button inserts data into a database.

```kotlin
class AccountActivity :
          AppCompatActivity() {

   val dbHandler = AccountDatabase(
                this@AccountActivity)

   override fun onCreate(
     savedInstanceState: Bundle?
   ){

     super.onCreate(savedInstanceState)

     setContentView(
           R.layout.account_activity)

     findViewById<Button>(
      R.id.next_screen_btn)
      .setOnClickListener {

       startActivity(
         Intent(this,
         AcctDetailsActivity::class.java)
           )
     }

     findViewById<Button>(
        R.id.save_user_data_button)
        .setOnClickListener {

          val userName = "Account#1"
          val location = "Sydney"
          val destination = "France"
```

```
dbHandler.
        insertUserDetails(
                username,
                location,
                destination)
```

Module#2 – Account Details Class

AcctDetailsActivity is the Activity that we are expecting once a user has navigated from AccountActivity.

```kotlin
class AcctDetailsActivity :
            AppCompatActivity() {

override fun onCreate(
    savedInstanceState: Bundle?
){

  super.onCreate(savedInstanceState)
  setContentView(
      R.layout.acct_details_activity)

    findViewById(R.id.details_txt)
          .text = "Acct Details"
  }
}
```

Module#3 - Database Class

```kotlin
class AccountDatabase(
    context: Context?
):SQLiteOpenHelper(
    context,
    DB_NAME,
    null,
    DB_VERSION)
{

    override fun onCreate(
        db:SQLiteDatabase
    ) {...}

    override fun onUpgrade(
        db: SQLiteDatabase,
        olderVersion: Int,
        newVersion: Int) {...}

    fun insertUserDetails(
        name: String?,
        location: String?,
        destination: String?
    ){
        val db = this.writableDatabase

        val cValues = contentValues()
```

```
        cValues.put(KEY_DEST, destination)

        db.insert(TABLE_USERS, null,
                cValues)
        db.close()

    }
}
```

Testing Integration Test - Robolectric

As stated above, integration testing is when individual software modules are combined and tested as a group.

src/test/AccountActivityTest.kt

```
@RunWith(RobolectricTestRunner::class)
class AccountActivityTest {

    private lateinit var activity :
                        AccountActivity

    private lateinit var dbHandler:
                        AccountDatabase
```

```kotlin
@Before
fun setup() {
 activity= Robolectric.setupActivity(
             AccountActivity::class)

 dbHandler = activity.dbHandler
}

@Test
fun shouldNotBeNull() {
  assertNotNull(activity)
}

@Test
fun clickBtn_shouldNavigateDetails() {

 activity.findViewById<Button>
   (R.id.next_screen_btn)
   .performClick()

 val expectedIntent = Intent(
    activity,
    AcctDetailsActivity::class.java
    )

  val actualIntent = shadowOf(
   RuntimeEnvironment
    .application
    .nextStartedActivity

  assertEquals(
     expectedIntent.getComponent(),
     actual.component)
```

```kotlin
@Test
fun verifyDatabaseIsEmpty() {
  assertEquals(
    dbHandler.getUsers().isEmpty(),
    true)
}

@Test
fun clickUserDataButn_
      dataBaseShouldNotBeEmpty() {

  activity.findViewById<Button>
        (R.id.save_user_data_button)
        .performClick()

  assertEqual(
      dbHandler.GetUsers().isEmpty(),
      false)
  }

}
```

Understanding Integration Test - Robolectric

The robolectric Test above includes the following:

1. *setup()* method:

    a) Inside the setup() method, we initialize common objects needed during our tests.

    b) We use the *@Before* annotation for setting up the Activity, and this annotation is possible because of the JUnit dependency added.

    c) *Robolectric.setupActivity()* launch activity in the resumed state and is ready and visible for the User to interact with.

    d) *dbHandler*: we grab the *dbHandler* instantiation to test how the database interacts with Activity.

```kotlin
@Before
fun setUp() {
    activity =
            Robolectric.setupActivity
            (AccountActivity::class.java)

    dbHandler = activity.dbHandler
}
```

2. Once the *setup()* function runs, as it should be the first to run since it has the @Before annotation, this Test will run and verify whether the Activity is null. If everything is correct in the setup method, then this should pass as the Activity should have

started.

```kotlin
@Test
fun shouldNotBeNull() {
    assertNotNull(activity)
}
```

3. In this case, clicking on the button is supposed to navigate the User to the next screen.

   Then we check if the expected result matches the actual results.

```kotlin
@Test
fun clickBtn_shouldNavigateDetails() {

  activity.findViewById<Button>
    (R.id.next_screen_btn)
    .performClick()

  val expectedIntent = Intent(
    activity,
    AcctDetailsActivity::class.java
  )
```

```
    val actualIntent = shadowOf(
      RuntimeEnvironment
      .application
      .nextStartedActivity

    assertEquals(
        expectedIntent.getComponent(),
        actual.component)
}
```

4. Upon *AccountActivity* starting, the database should be initially empty. The Test below verifies that the database is empty.

```
@Test
fun verifyDatabaseIsEmpty() {
  assertEquals(
      dbHandler.getUsers().isEmpty(),
      true)
}
```

5. Once the *User* clicks on the *user_data_button*, the database is accessed and data inserted. The Test below, verify that the database is not empty.

```kotlin
@Test
fun clickUserDataButn_
    dataBaseShouldNotBeEmpty() {

  activity.findViewById<Button>
      (R.id.save_user_data_button)
      .performClick()

  assertEqual(
      dbHandler.GetUsers().isEmpty(),
      false)
}
```

Table 4: Robolectric Annotations Table

`@Config(sdk = { JELLY_BEAN, JELLY_BEAN_MR1 })`	
Robolectric will run based on the specified SDK target. Specifying the SDK enables the code to run under that particular SDK version.	
`... @Config(sdk = KITKAT) fun runOnKitKat() { } ...`	
A particular method can also run on a specific SDK target.	
`@Config(application = MyOtherApplication::class) class MyAccountTest`	
Robolectric will instantiate the default application class; however, a custom application class will be run to replace the default.	

Chapter Summary

The idea behind integration testing is to combine modules in the application and test them as a group to see that they are working fine. Integrated Testing helps simulate the interaction between various modules and how well the module integrates with the Android API framework.

Robolectric occurs after unit testing.

Android official Testing library includes Robolectric. The next chapter speaks on AndroidX | Robolectric.

Chapter Five: Integration Tests (Androidx | Robolectric)

MEDIUM TESTS
Androidx | Robolectric

Androidx

Androidx stands for Android Extension Library. The Androidx namespace comprises the Android Jetpack libraries. Jetpack provides backward compatibility as Each Android version has different capabilities and new additions. Support library allows applications to be compatible across all the versions of Android that are released. The focus with Androidx is on the changes to Testing.

Androidx | Robolectric

Robolectric version 4 and higher is compatible with Android's official testing libraries. AndroidX Test is the new way of testing code that interacts with the Android framework. Through Robolectric, Androidx can run tests on the JVM, emulator, or real devices. Below example, run the JVM tests, as the execution time for the Test improved massively.

Robolecgric uses *Robolectric.setupActivity* API to start the activity lifecycle state for Testing. Androidx uses ActivityScenario and ActivityScenarioRule. which provides APIs to start and drive an Activity's lifecycle state for Testing. Section 1 and 2 speak on ActivityScenario and ActivityScenarioRule, respectively. Section 3 focuses on Testing Fragments (FragmentScenario).

Section 1: Testing Activity

with ActivityScenario

ActivityScenario has complete control over the state of the Activity. We can test the application in different states, such as *onCreate*(), *onResume*(), and the other lifecycle methods. It is possible to run on either the JVM or on a device.

build.gradle

```
android {
   ...
   testOptions.unitTests
       .includeAndroidResources = true
   ...
}

dependencies {

  testImplementation
  'org.robolectric:robolectric:<version>'

  testImplementation
     'androidx.test.ext.junit:<version>'
}
```

Testing Integration Test - Androidx | Robolectric

The Test below is the same as the Robolectric Test in chapter 4 using Androidx API.

src/test/AccountActivityTest.kt

```kotlin
@RunWith(AndroidJUnit4::class)
class AccountActivityTest {

    private lateinit var scenario :
        ActivityScenario<AccountActivity>

    private lateinit var dbHandler:
                        AccountDatabase

    @Before
    fun setup() {
      scenario =
          ActivityScenario.launch(
            AccountActivity::class.java)

      scenario.moveToState(
            Lifecycle.State.CREATED)
    }

    @After
    fun cleanup() {
      scenario.close()
```

```kotlin
@Test
fun shouldNotBeNull() {
  scenario.onActivity { activity ->
    Assert.assertNotNull(activity)
  }
}

@Test
fun clickButton_should
    NavigateToAccountDetailsActivity() {
  scenario.onActivity { activity ->

    activity.findViewById<Button>(
        R.id.next_screen_btn)
        .performClick()

    val expectedIntent = Intent(
        activity,
    AccountDetailsActivity::class.java)

    val actual = Shadows.shadowOf(
        RuntimeEnvironment.application)
        .nextStartedActivity

    Assert.assertEquals(
        expectedIntent.component,
                actual.component)

  }
}
```

```kotlin
@Test
fun verifyDatabaseIsEmpty() {
  scenario.onActivity { activity ->
    dbHandler = activity.dbHandler

  Assert.assertEquals(
    dbHandler.GetUsers().isEmpty(),
    true)
  }
}

@Test
fun clickUserDataButton_
      dataBaseShouldNotBeEmpty() {
  scenario.onActivity { activity ->
    dbHandler = activity.dbHandler

  activity.findViewById<Button>(
    R.id.save_user_data_button)
  .performClick()

  Assert.assertEquals(
    dbHandler.GetUsers().isEmpty(),
    false)
  }
 }
}
```

Understanding Integration Test
- Androidx | Robolectric

Since the Test is build using JUnit 4, we must explicitely tag the class with @RunWith(AndroidJUnit4::class)

```kotlin
@RunWith(AndroidJUnit4::class)
```

The *setup()* method is the first method called, and it runs before each test runs because of the @Before annotation.

ActivityScenarios allows us to create the Activity; therefore, we do just that with *ActivityScenario.launch*

```kotlin
@Before
fun setup() {
    scenario =
        ActivityScenario.launch(
            AccountActivity::class.java)

    scenario.moveToState(
            Lifecycle.State.CREATED)
}
```

3. Once we have a reference to the scenario, we transition the Activity to the desired state by using the *moveToState(state)* method, which allows the following transitions:

```
scenario.moveToState(Lifecycle.State.CREATED)
```

```
scenario.moveToState(Lifecycle.State.STARTED)
```

```
scenario.moveToState(Lifecycle.State.RESUMED)
```

```
scenario.moveToState(Lifecycle.State.DESTROYED)
```

4. Once we are in the desired state, we can proceed to test using an assertion such as:

```
scenario.onActivity { activity ->
    Assert.assertNotNull(activity)
}
```

5. ActivityScenrio does not automatically clean up the device state and may leave the Activity running after the test finishes. Call close() to clean up the state.

```
@After
fun cleanup() {
  scenario.close()
}
```

Section 2: Testing Activity with ActivityScenarioRule

ActivityScenarios does not clean up the state that the Activity is in upon a completed test. There is the need to have a method that does that. The close()method cleans up the activity state.

```kotlin
@After
fun cleanup() {
    scenario.close()
}
```

With *ActivityScenarioRules*, there is no need to clean up the state, as that happens automatically. *ActivityScenarioRules* launches an activity before the Test begins and closes after the Test completes; this is an updated version of ActivityTestRule, which is now deprecated.

Testing with *activityScenarioRule* is as follows

src/test/AccountActivityTest.kt

```kotlin
@RunWith(AndroidJUnit4::class)
class AccountActivityTest {

@get:Rule
var rule: ActivityScenarioRule
                <AccountActivity> =
    ActivityScenarioRule(
        AccountActivity::class.java)

private lateinit var scenario :
    ActivityScenario<AccountActivity>

private lateinit var dbHandler:
                    AccountDatabase

@Before
fun setup() {
  scenario = rule.scenario
}

@Test
fun shouldNotBeNull() {
  scenario.onActivity { activity ->
     Assert.assertNotNull(activity)
  }
}
```

```kotlin
@Test
fun clickButton_should
  NavigateToAccountDetailsActivity() {

  scenario.onActivity { activity ->

  activity.findViewById<Button>(
        R.id.next_screen_btn)
        .performClick()

  val expectedIntent =Intent(
    activity,
    AccountDetailsActivity::class.java)

  val actual = Shadows.shadowOf(
     RuntimeEnvironment.application)
     .nextStartedActivity

  Assert.assertEquals(
      expectedIntent.component,
                  actual.component)
  }
}

@Test
fun verifyDatabaseIsEmpty() {
  scenario.onActivity { activity ->
    dbHandler = activity.dbHandler

  Assert.assertEquals(
    dbHandler.GetUsers().isEmpty(),
    true)
  }
}
```

```kotlin
@Test
fun clickUserDataButton_
    dataBaseShouldNotBeEmpty() {
  scenario.onActivity { activity ->
    dbHandler = activity.dbHandler

    activity.findViewById<Button>(
        R.id.save_user_data_button)
        .performClick()

    Assert.assertEquals(
       dbHandler.GetUsers().isEmpty(),
       false)
  }
 }
}
```

ActivityScenarioRule launches the Activity before the Test starts and closes the Activity after the Test completes.

```kotlin
@get:Rule
var rule: ActivityScenarioRule
                <AccountActivity> =
    ActivityScenarioRule(
        AccountActivity::class.java)

private lateinit var scenario :
    ActivityScenario<AccountActivity>

...

@Before
fun setup() {
   scenario = rule.scenario
}
...
```

Section 3: Testing Fragments (FragmentScenario)

Launching an activity housing a fragment means that you are not testing that Fragment in isolation — a test should only care about that Fragment itself and not the parent containers. FragmentScenario has complete control over the state of the Fragment. We can test the Fragment in different *states*, such as *onCreate()*, *onResume()*, and the other lifecycle methods. It is possible to run on either the JVM or on a device. FragmentScenario only tests the androidx fragment class.

build.gradle

```
dependencies {
  debugImplementation(
    "androidx.fragment:fragment-testing:<version>")

  debugImplementation(
      "androidx.test:runner:<version>")

  testImplementation(
      "androidx.test.ext:junit:<version>")

  testImplementation(
      "org.robolectric:robolectric:
```

FragmentScenarios Testing

Assuming we have a fragment called *AccountFragment*. Testing with *FragmentScenario* is as follows

*src/test/*AccountFragmentTest.*kt*

```kotlin
@RunWith(AndroidJUnit4::class)
class AccountFragmentTest {

    val scenario =
        FragmentScenario.launch(
            FirstFragment::class.java)

    @Before
    fun setup() {
        scenario.moveState(
            Lifecycle.State.STARTED)
    }

    @Test
    fun shouldNotBeNull {
        scenario.onFragment { frag -> {
            Assert.assertNotNull(frag)
        }
    }
}
```

Understanding FragmentScenarios

Step 1: Create the Fragment by calling the launch() function.

```kotlin
val scenario =
    FragmentScenario.launch(
        FirstFragment::class.java)
```

Instead of using the *launch()* method, another option is to use the *launchInContainer()*method; Which takes in arguments such as a Bundle, theme id, Lifecycle state, and fragment factory.

FragmentScenario has a function called *recreate()* function, which allows you to recreate the Fragment state if you want to.

```
Scenario.recreate()
```

Step 2: Move the state

Once we have a reference to the scenario, we transition the Fragment to the desired state by using *the moveToState(state)* method, which allows the following transitions:

```kotlin
scenario.moveToState(Lifecycle.State.CREATED)
```

```kotlin
scenario.moveToState(Lifecycle.State.STARTED)
```

```kotlin
scenario.moveToState(Lifecycle.State.RESUMED)
```

```kotlin
scenario.moveToState(Lifecycle.State.DESTROYED)
```

Step 3: Having access to the scenario allows access to the Fragment, and we can then proceed to test functionalities of interest.

```
scenario.onFragment { frag -> {
    Assert.assertNotNull(frag)
}
```

Chapter Summary

Robolectric allows Android applications to test on the JVM without an emulator or device.

Integration testing is testing where software modules are combined and tested as a group.

Integration testing exposes and detects defects in the interaction bewteen modules.

The following section focuses on Large Testing, known as UI test. *Large* test cases deal with the interaction between modules, activities and mimic real-world scenarios.

PART IV: LARGE TESTS

User Interface Testing

User Interface or functional Testing falls under that category of large tests. Large tests focus on how the modules interact with one another and the system as a whole. Large Testing covers the look and feel of the application and mimics real-world scenarios.

These tests do not concern themselves with the internal logic of the software. The purpose of UI testing is to remove poor user experiences when interacting with the app. User Interface testing aims to increase the code's confidence, e.g., the button clicked's functionality, whether a view is at a specified location, etc.

Android Test Tools

LARGE TESTS
Espresso,
Androidx | Espresso

Espresso

Espresso Test Library is a testing framework for Android to make it easy to write reliable user interface tests. Espresso is customizable, automated, and ensures only one assertion can occur at any time. The tests run on an emulator or actual device.

Androidx | Espresso

Espresso is compatible with Android official testing libraries. Chapter 7 focuses on Espresso when it comes to androidx, as Androidx Test is the new way of testing code that interacts with the Android framework.

Chapter Six: User Interface Tests (Espresso)

Espresso

Espresso framework, released by Google, is used to write User Interface tests. The framework starts the Activity before every test run. Espresso runs on real devices or emulators. This Testing is known as instrumentation testing.

Espresso is synchronous, meaning it waits for user interface events in the current message queue to process before moving to the next operation, so no need to add timing workarounds.

Espresso has three essential components:
1. **ViewMatchers** – Find the View in the current hierarchy
2. **ViewActions** – Act on a view
3. **ViewAssertions** – Verify expected behavior

The basics of an espresso test are as follows:

```
onView(ViewMarcher)
        .perform(ViewAction)
            .check(ViewAssertion)
```

- Find the View
- Act on the View
- Make/Validate an assertion

Espresso Setup

The Espresso testing framework is part of the Android Support library. The next chapter speaks on the latest changes to the said statement.

app/build.gradle file and add the following:

```groovy
android {
    ...
    defaultConfig {
        testInstrumentationRunner
                "android.support.test.runner.AndroidJUnitRunner"
    }
}

dependencies {
    testImplementation
            'Junit:junit:<version>'

    androidTestImplementation
        'com.android.support.test:runner:<version>'
    androidTestImplementation
        'com.android.support.test.espresso:
```

Unit Under Test

Let's say we have the following layout to test, containing a TextView and a Button. We will use Espresso to verify that TextView correctly displays the "*My Account*" on the device screen.
account_activity.xml

```xml
<?xml version="1.0" encoding="utf-8"?>
<LinearLayout
    xmlns:android=
        "http://schemas.android.com/apk/res/android"
    android:orientation="vertical"
    android:layout_width="match_parent"
    android:layout_height="match_parent">

    <TextView
        android:id="@+id/account_title
        android:layout_width="wrap_content"
        android:layout_height=

            "wrap_content"
        android:layout_gravity="center"
        android:textSize="18sp"
        android:text="My Accounts"/>

    <Button
        android:id="@+id/next_screen_btn"
        android:layout_width="wrap_content"
        android:layout_height=

            "wrap_content"
        android:layout_gravity="center"
```

Testing Unit Under Test

AccountActivityUiTest::class

```kotlin
@RunWith(AndroidJUnit4::class)
class AccountActivityUiTest {

  @Rule @JvmField var
      activityActivityTestRule =
          ActivityTestRule(
              MainActivity::class.java)

  @Before
  fun setup() {}

  @Test
  fun verifyActivityTitleTest() {
      onView(withId(R.id.account_title))
         .check(matches(
             withText("My Accounts")))
  }
```

Testing User Interface

1. *ActivityScenarioRule*

```
@Rule @JvmField var
        activityActivityTestRule =
            ActivityTestRule(
                MainActivity::class.java)
```

ActivityTestRule is used to create and launch the Activity under Test before each Test and close it after each Test completes.

2. The TextView can be verified as follows:

```
onView(withId(R.id.account_title))
        .check(matches(
            withText("My Accounts")))
```

- Espresso finds the View via viewMatcher -> *withId()*
- An action is perform with the *check()* method call
- Validated with *matches(withText())*

Chapter Summary

A basic skeleton code of an Espresso Test is:

onView(*ViewMatcher*).perform(*ViewAction*).check(*ViewAssertion*)

- *ViewMatchers* – allows us to find a view in the view hierarchy.
- *ViewActions* – Perform automated actions on the View.
- *ViewAssertions* – allows us to assert the state of the View.

Chapter Seven: User Interface Tests (Androidx | Espresso)

Espresso tests are instrumentation testing. It runs on an actual device or emulator and behaves like a real user using the app. Espresso is synchronous; it detects when the main thread is idle and waits for user interface events. With such capability, there is no need to add timing workarounds.

Espresso has three essential components:

1. **ViewMatchers** - Find the view in the current hierarchy.

2. **ViewActions** - Act on a view.

3. **ViewAssertions** - Verify expected behavior.

The basics of an espresso test are as follows:

```
onView(ViewMarcher)
        .perform(ViewAction)
            .check(ViewAssertion)
```

- Find the View
- Act on the View
- Make/Validate an assertion

Espresso Setup

Setting up the Espresso Framework in the Androidx environment is as follows. With *AndroidJUnitRunner* class is needed to run instrumentation tests, and JUnit and Espresso testing frameworks are the dependencies.

app/build.gradle file and add the following:

```
android {
    defaultConfig {
        testInstrumentationRunner
                    "androidx.test.runner.AndroidJUnitRunner"
    }
}

dependencies {
    androidTestImplementation
        'androidx.test.ext:junit:<version>'

    androidTestImplementation
            'androidx.test.espresso:espresso-
```

Testing User Interface

AccountActivityUiTest::class

```kotlin
@RunWith(AndroidJUnit4::class)
class AccountActivityUiTest {

    @get:Rule var activityScenarioRule =
        activityScenarioRule<MainActivity>()

    @Test
    fun verifyActivityTitleTest() {

        onView(withId(R.id.account_title))
            .check(matches(withText("My Accounts")))
    }
}
```

Testing User Interface

ActivityScenarioRule

```
@get:Rule var activityScenarioRule =
        activityScenarioRule<MainActivity>()
```

ActivityScenarioRule is used to create and launch the Activity under Test before each Test and close it after each Test completes.

The *TextView* can be verified as follows:

```
onView(withId(R.id.account_title)).check(
    matches(withText("My Accounts"))
)
```

- Espresso finds the View via viewMatcher -> withId()
- An action is perform with the *check()* method call
- Validated with *matches(withText())*

ViewMatchers

The purpose of the matcher is to match a view using different attributes. With the onView() method, we can use these attributes to match and find views. Some views can be referenced by ID, while a text can reference others it contains or a hint, even *contentDescription* of the View. The table below shows frequently used ViewMatchers.

Table 5. Commonly Used Viewmatchers

onData(withText("Hello World")).atPosition(7)
onData() is used to test Recyclerview, ListView, Adapter, and GridView.
onView(R.id.btnView)
Finds a view with the resource id.
onView(WithText("*end*"))
Finds a view with the word *end*.
onView(withContentDescription("senses"))
Finds a view with the content description of senses.
onView(withHint("sample hint"))
Searches for a view with a hint.
onView(withSpinnerText("spinner"))
Locates a spinner with a text *spinner*.
onView(allOf(withId(R.id.myid), isDisplayed()))
Makes sure that the View is displayed; if not, then fail the Test.
onView(allOf(withId(R.id.myid), isClickable()))
Verifies the View is clickable; if not, then fails the Test.

onView(allOf(withId(R.id.myid), isCompletelyDisplayed()))

Verifies the View is displayed on the screen; if not, then fail the Test.

onView(allOf(withId(R.id.myid), isChecked()))

Applies to compound buttons or any subtype of it with a checked state.

onView(allOf(withId(R.id.myid), isNotChecked()))

Verifies the View is not checked; if not, then Test fails.

onView(allOf(withId(R.id.myid), isEnabled()))

Makes sure that it is enabled; if not, then it fails the Test.

onView(allOf(withId(R.id.myid), hasFocus()))

Verifies that the View has focus; if not, then fails the Test.

onView(allOf(withId(R.id.myid), hasLinks()))

Returns a matcher having links.
Applies to TextView only.

onView(allOf(withId(R.id.myid), isSelected()))

Verifies the View is selected; if not, then fails the Test.

onView(allOf(withId(R.id.myid), hasContentDescription()))

Verifies the View has a content description; if not, then fails the Test.

onView(withText(*startsWith*("World")))

Verifies whether the actual input starts with a specified string.

ViewActions

Once *onView()* or *onData()* Espresso's ViewMatcher method finds the view. ViewActions is responsible for providing the interaction that we would like to occur on the View during Testing.

Table 6: Viewactions Commonly Used:

onView(R.id.btn_view).*perform(click())* onView(R.id.btn_view).perform(doubleClick()) onView(R.id.btn_view). perform(longClick())
Perform click actions on a view.
onView(withText("*end*")).*perform(replaceText("start"))* onView(withText("*end*")). perform(cleartext()) onView(withText("*end*")).perform(typeText("Hello"))
Replaces the text *end* with the word *start*.
onView(withId(R.id.nav_view)).*perform(swipeUp())* onView(withId(R.id.nav_view)).perform(swipeDown()) onView(withId(R.id.nav_view)).perform(swipeLeft()) onView(withId(R.id.nav_view)).perform(swipeRight())
Swiping actions on a view.
onView(withId(R.id.list_view)).*perform(scrollTo())*

Scrolls a ListView.
onView(withId(R.id.text_view)).*perform(typeText("Hello", pressKey(KeyEvent.KEYCODE_ENTER)))* onView(withId(R.id.text_view)).perform(pressImeActionButton())
Types a text into the View, then presses the key event specified.
onView(withId(R.id.btn_view)).*perform(pressBack())*
Triggers the back button.

Custom *ViewActions* are also implemented by using *ViewAction*, which contains three methods:

- getConstraints()

    Returns a *Matcher<View>*

- getDescription()

    Returns any string you want.

- perform(uiController: UiController, view: View)

    Used to do your custom logic.

ViewAssertions

View assertion asserts that both the actual View and the expected views are the same. View assertions should not conduct any blocking operations, as it runs on the UI thread.

Assertions make sure that the app shows the correct UI as expected and completes the Espresso test cases.

Table 7: Viewassertion Table

onView(withId(R.id.btn)).*check*(matches(isDisplayed()))   onView(withId(R.id.btn)).*check*(matches(withText("hello")))   onView(withId(R.id.btn)).*check*(matches(withText(R.string.hello)))
Checks the element is displayed.
onView(withId(R.id.view)).*check*(isBottomAlignedWith(withId(R.id.target_view)))   onView(withId(R.id.view)).*check*(isCompletelyAbove(withId(R.id.target_view)))   onView(withId(R.id.view)).*check*(isCompletelyBelow(withId(R.id.target_view)))   onView(withId(R.id.view)).*check*(isCompletelyLeftOf(withId(R.id.target_view)))

onView(withId(R.id.view)).*check*(isCompletelyRightOf(withId(R.id.target_view)))	
Verifies the View exists at the bottom of the specified location of the target view matcher specified.	
onView(withId(R.id.view)).*check*(isLeftAlignedWith(withId(R.id.target_view)))	
onView(withId(R.id.view)).*check*(isRightAlignedWith(withId(R.id.target_view)))	
onView(withId(R.id.view)).*check*(isTopAlignedWith(withId(R.id.target_view)))	
onView(withId(R.id.view)).*check*(isPartiallyAbove(withId(R.id.target_view)))	
onView(withId(R.id.view)).*check*(isPartiallyBelow(withId(R.id.target_view)))	
onView(withId(R.id.view)).*check*(isParticallyLeftOf(withId(R.id.target_view)))	
onView(withId(R.id.view)).*check*(isPartiallyRightOf(withId(R.id.target_view)))	
Ensures the View exists to the left, right, top, or below of the target view.	

Chapter Summary

Espresso tests are instrumentation testing; it runs on an actual device or emulator and behaves as if a real user uses the app. Espresso is synchronous, and it detects when the main thread is idle and waits for user interface events.

Espresso catches bugs in the user interactions, thus improving the overall experience. Testing the app ensures that users don't encounter unexpected results.

A basic skeleton code of an Espresso Test is:

onView(***ViewMatcher***).perform(***ViewAction***).check(***ViewAssertion***)

- *ViewMatchers*
    allows us to find a view in the view hierarchy.
- *ViewActions*
    Perform automated actions on the View.
- *ViewAssertions* –
    allows us to assert the state of the View.

CONCLUSION

A codebase that has adequate Testing will have fewer errors and attract more users. Good Testing is a combination of Small, Medium, and Large Testing.

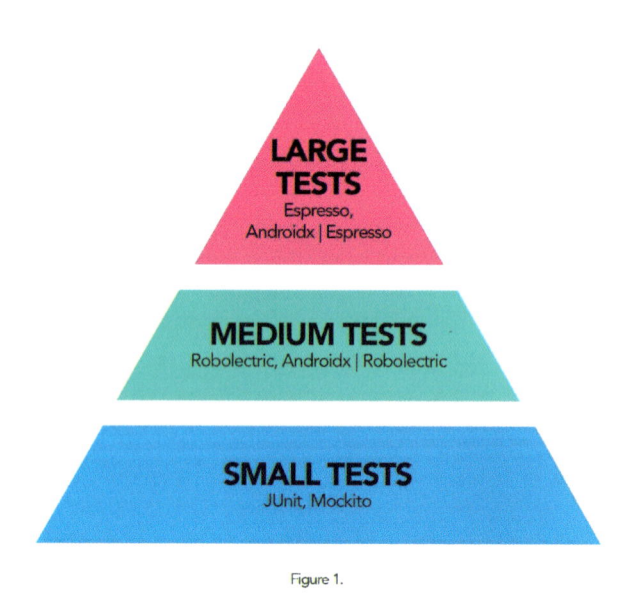

Figure 1.

Small Testing is a testing method by which we verify individual and independent units of source code. In contrast, Medium Testing checks integration between modules. A Large test deals with user interface testing, testing an interface to verify the expected result.

Small (Unit) Unit Testing tests each part of the program and shows that the individual pieces are correct. JUnit and Mockito frameworks cover unit testing.

Medium (Integration) Integration Testing combines different modules in the application and Tests as a group to see they are working fine. Robolectric is the go-to for integration testing in Android.

Large (UI) Testing means testing a vertical slice of functionality in the system (may interact with dependencies) to confirm that the code yields expected behavior for the end-user. Espresso covers these types of Testing.

Lastly, the ratio of the small, medium and large tests should roughly follow the following criteria:
1. Small tests 70–80%
2. Medium tests 10–20%
3. Large tests 5–10 %

ACKNOWLEDGMENTS

"No one-not rock stars, not professional athletes, not software billionaires, and not even geniuses-ever makes it alone."

— Malcolm Gladwell, Outliers: The Story of Success

I want to shout out to everyone who has helped me along the way. From my editors, Yaseen AlDallash and Yegor Lus, thank you. Special thanks to Tanya Remfort, my proofreaders, and Andy Meaden, the most outstanding book cover designer.

EDITORS

Yaseen AlDallash is a software engineer with a bachelor's degree in Mechatronics Engineering from Higher Tech. Institute. His work focused on re-architecting and creating different features with modular, reusable, high efficient, and efficiently testable aspects in mind during his career. His Mechatronics engineering background and passion for biomimicry inspired him to bring innovative solutions to software engineering.

Yegor Lus is a software engineer in the DevOps space. He lives in New York with his wife and two kids. He graduated from NYU, after which he was a Test Engineer at three companies before transitioning to Enigma Technologies, where he is currently Head of DevOps. He is known to practice the Aikido martial art. He enjoys all things geek ranging from Lord of the Rings to The Expanse.

ABOUT THE AUTHOR

Marc Daniel Registre is an Electrical Engineer by education but a Software Engineer by profession. Upon graduating from NYU, he worked as an Aerospace Engineer before transitioning to developing mobile applications used by millions. Marc lives in New York with his wife Christina and man best friend, Milo. As should all right-thinking people, he enjoys avocado. Buy this book, and you'll learn to test in less than a week.